Reflections for Organ

Gilbert M. Martin

Reflections for Organ

by Gilbert M. Martin

Table of Contents

Distributed by Antara Music Group

Reflections for Organ

I Morning Song

Sw. Accompaniment Stops (8′)
Gt. Solo Stop
Ped. Light 16′, Sw. to Ped. 8′

Gilbert M. Martin

BG0865

rit.
a tempo
Sw.
Gt.

II Berceuse

Sw. String Celeste 8′, Flute 4′
Gt. Keen Solo Stop 8′
Ped. Light 16′

Gilbert M. Martin

BG0865

a tempo
Gt. mf
rall.
cresc.
f
mf

rit.
Tempo primo
Sw. (–Flute 8')
mp
Gt.
mf
rall.

a tempo
Sw.
rit.

III A Quiet Prayer

Sw. String 8′, 4′
Gt. Light Diapason 8′
Ped. Light 16′, Sw. to Ped. 8′

Gilbert M. Martin

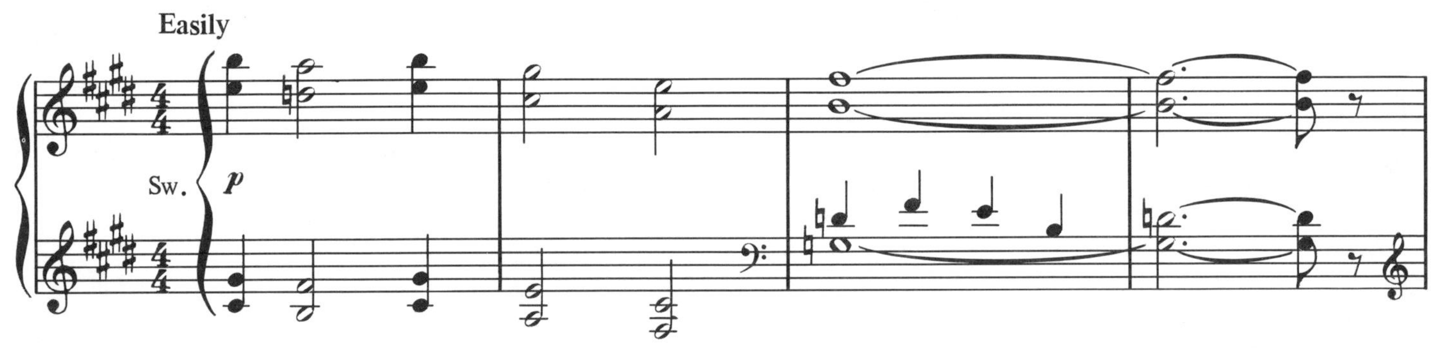

Moderately

espr.

rit.

1.

2.

rit.

As at start
Sw.
p
rall.
a tempo
p
pp

IV Grace and Thanks

Sw. Flute 8′, 4′ (String 4′)
Gt. Light Diapason 8′
Ped. Bourdon 16′, Sw. to Ped. 8′

Gilbert M. Martin

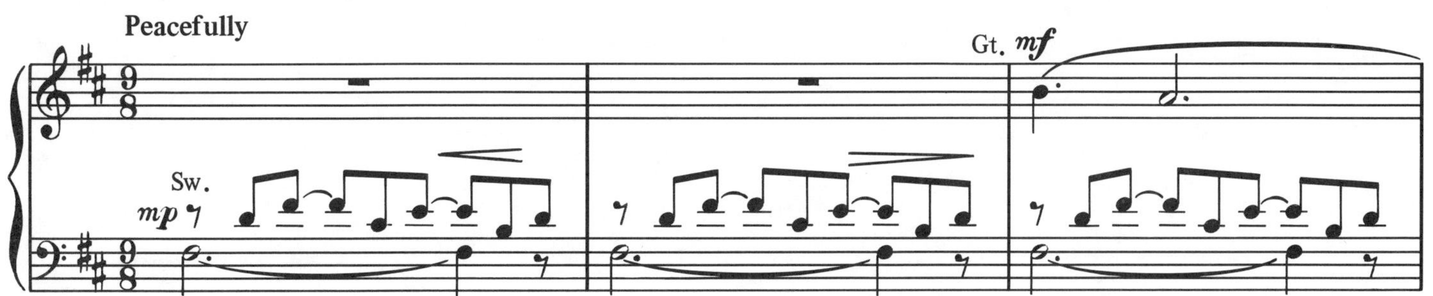

più f
dim. e rit.
a tempo
mp

a tempo
rit.
Sw. (+String 8′)
mp
Gt. (Gamba 8′) mf

f
più f
dim.
mf
mp
Slowly
mp
p

V Sweet Adoration

Sw. String Celeste 8', 4'
Gt. Flute 8' (2')
Ped. Light 16', Sw. to Ped. 8'

Gilbert M. Martin

BG0865

Gt. Light Reed 8′
mf
(Sw.)
mp
cresc.
f
mf
rit.

As at start
Gt. Light Diapason 8'
mp
3
mf
espr.

rall.
a tempo
mf
rit.
a tempo

VI Chorale and Laud

Sw. Light Diapason 8′, Flute 4′
Gt. Solo Stop 8′
Ped. Light 16′, 8′

Gilbert M. Martin

Rather slowly; reverently

Sw. *mp* *espr.*

Moderately

cresc.
poco
a
poco

f
ff
f
dim.
poco
a
poco

mf
f
mp
mf
p
mp